Lost Railways of Co. 'Derry

by
Stephen Johnson

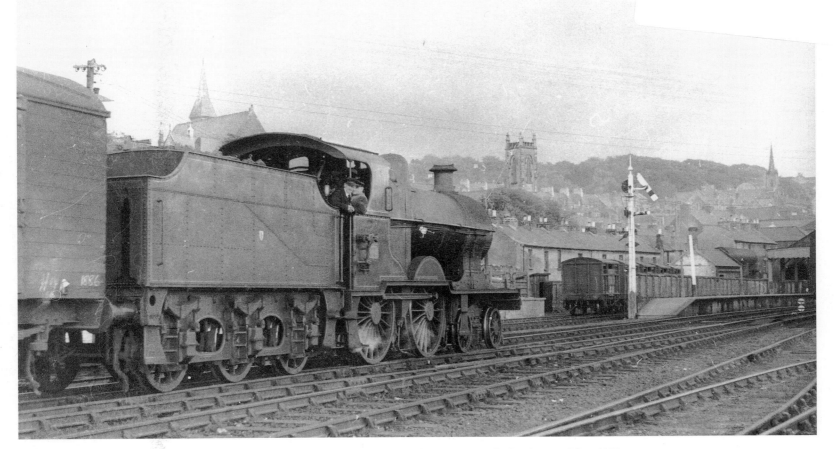

UTA U2 Class 4-4-0, No. 77, at Londonderry Waterside Station, 19 May 1950.

PICTURE ACKNOWLEDGEMENTS
The publishers wish to thank the following for contributing pictures to this book: John Alsop for pages 24, 26 and 27; R.M. Casserley for the inside front cover, pages 1, 2, 7, 13, 15, 17, 19–22, 28–31, 34–42, 45, 47, 48, the inside back cover and the back cover (with the exceptions of those on pages 7, 28 and 45, all of these photographs were taken by H.C. Casserley); and Ian McCullough for the front cover and pages 4–6, 8–12, 14, 16, 18, 23, 25, 32, 44 and 46. The pictures on pages 33 and 43 are from the publishers' collection.

GNR(I) Qs Class 4-4-0, No. 135, 'Cyclops', heads the 4.00 p.m. departure from Londonderry Foyle Road to Belfast Great Victoria Street, 6 August 1930.

INTRODUCTION

The county of 'Derry once had an extensive railway network of both broad and narrow gauge lines, with Londonderry once boasting four stations, two broad and two narrow gauge. Sadly, there are now just two lines remaining, one from Belfast to Londonderry via Coleraine, and the Portrush branch. The main operator in the county was the Northern Counties Committee (NCC) of the British London Midland and Scottish Railway (LMS). The LMS involvement in Northern Ireland came about in 1903 when the English Midland Railway (MR), keen to extend its empire, bought the Belfast and Northern Counties Railway (BNCR). The 1924 groupings of English railway companies led to the formation of the 'Big Fā}r', with the MR becoming part of the newly formed LMS. The British influence could clearly be seen, especially in terms of locomotive and rolling stock designs, many being based on MR and LMS types, although modified for use on the Irish standard gauge of 5 feet 3 inches. Apart from the main Belfast – Londonderry route, the NCC also operated a number of other lines including the Derry Central Railway which ran from Magherafelt to Macfin. This was part of a larger and more ambitious plan, but in the event only this section was built and the line remained a backwater. Cookstown had the distinction of being served by both the NCC and GNR(I). Branch lines to the plantation towns of Draperstown and Dungiven were built with the support of the Draper's Company and the Skinner's Company respectively, but these were never profitable lines and lost their services in the 1930s.

The NCC also operated two 3 feet gauge railways in the county. The Donegal Railway Company built an extension from Strabane to Londonderry Victoria Road, which opened in 1900. After the joint purchase of the Donegal Railway Company by the MR NCC and the GNR(I), the Government handed this extension to the NCC in order to avoid a monopoly of the route from Londonderry to Strabane by the GNR(I). The other was the short lived Portstewart Tramway which was built in an effort to serve the resort of Portstewart after the broad gauge line had bypassed the town on its way to Portrush.

The NCC became part of the Ulster Transport Authority (UTA) on 1 April 1949. The UTA were not disposed to supporting loss-making lines and didn't waste much time in closing some of the remaining routes. The Derry Central and Cookstown branch were closed in 1950, with the Limavady branch and narrow gauge Strabane to Londonderry lines going in 1955.

The NCC was not the only operator serving the county. The Great Northern Railway of Ireland (GNR(I)) served Londonderry with two routes, one to Belfast and one to Dundalk and Dublin. However, only five miles of this route were actually in Co. 'Derry, running up the west bank of the River Foyle to Foyle Road Station. The GNR(I) was one of the few Irish railway companies to remain independent until closure. This was because all lines operating wholly within the Irish Free State became absorbed in the Great Southern Railways company (eventually to become CIE), while all those operating in the north eventually came under the control of the UTA; those lines that crossed over the international border, such as the GNR(I), remained independent.

The GNR(I) crossed the border no less than seventeen times and this situation ultimately caused the company's demise as services were hindered by customs checks and natural traffic flows were disrupted. The financial difficulties that this railway suffered in the 1930s came to a head in the 1950s and it had to be bailed out by the governments of the two countries; this led to the establishment of the Great Northern Railway Board in 1953. Disagreement over funding of the GNRB led to the Northern Government withdrawing from the arrangement, resulting in the wholesale closure of parts of the GNRB network, with the Clones to Londonderry section of the GNR(I) route closing in October 1957. The remaining part of the route to Londonderry from Belfast via Portadown passed to the UTA a year later with the dissolution of the GNRB. The Derry Road, as it was fondly known, survived under UTA control for another seven years, until it too closed on 15 February 1965.

The other major operator in Co. 'Derry was the Londonderry & Lough Swilly Railway. Only three miles or so of their 3 feet gauge railway was actually in Co. 'Derry, but from Graving Dock Station on the west bank of the River Foyle, north of the Londonderry GNR(I) station, this company operated services into the far reaches of Co. Donegal. The company started off as a 5 feet 3 inch broad gauge railway, but was narrowed in 1885. With a chequered history, the railway remained independent until closure in 1953. The Swilly also operated a number of bus services in the area and long after the closure of the railway, buses could still be seen sporting the company's logo!

As a busy sea port, the Londonderry Port and Harbour Commissioners (LP&HC) thought it advantageous to try and connect all these lines together with their docks. With only one bridge across the river and two different gauges on each side, the solution was to build a mixed gauge line. The lower deck of the Craigavon bridge was laid with a mixed 5 feet 3 inch and 3 feet line. As the bridge was at right angles to all the other lines, access was by means of wagon turntables at each end and, as such, locomotives were prohibited from using the bridge. The main part of the LP&HC mixed gauge lines ran up the west bank of the River Foyle and the Commissioners' locomotives were equipped with both broad gauge three link couplings and narrow gauge 'chopper' couplings which were slightly offset and lower on the buffer beam. With the demise of the main railways, the LP&HC closed their system in 1962.

In the course of this book the NCC system is examined first with its Cookstown branch and Derry Central lines before moving on to the company's branch lines and the Portstewart Tramway. The Great Northern Railway's route into the Maiden City follows and then there is an account of the Londonderry & Lough Swilly Railway. We finish with a look at the Londonderry Port and Harbour Commissioners dockside railway before finally looking at the closed passenger stations on the sole remaining main line and branch in the county. Please note that throughout the book the county town is named as Londonderry as this was how it was referred to on railway timetables.

Toome Bridge – Magherafelt and Cookstown *

Passenger service withdrawn	28 August 1950	*Stations closed*	*Date*
Distance	17.5 miles	Castledawson	28 August 1950
Company	Northern Counties Committee	Magherafelt	28 August 1950
		Moneymore	28 August 1950
* The closed station on this line that was in Co. Antrim was Toome Bridge.		Cookstown	28 August 1950

Castledawson Station, looking east. Opened in 1856 with the extension of the line from Randalstown to Cookstown, this was served by passenger trains until 1950, although goods services continued to use the line to Kilrea until 1959.

This line left the Northern Counties Committee Belfast to Londonderry main line at Cookstown Junction. The first part of the line ran through Randalstown and Toome Bridge and is covered in *Lost Railways of Co. Antrim*. The extension of the Randalstown branch to Cookstown was authorised by the Belfast & Ballymena Extension Act on 28 June 1853. Work started at Moneymore on 24 March 1855 and the line was to cross the Lower Bann at Toome Bridge. As the River Bann was used for navigation, a low lattice girder bridge with a swivel span was built. From here, the line carried on to Cookstown via Castledawson, Magherafelt and Moneymore. Construction was completed fairly quickly and the extension was inspected by the Board of Trade on 13 October 1856. They were not satisfied with the bridge at Toome which appears to have been of a temporary nature and, left with this and a few other problems, the Belfast & Ballymena Railway got to work and were ready again by the end of October.

Magherafelt Station, looking west from the footbridge, with NCC A1 Class 4-4-0, No. 65, 'Knockagh', at the up platform. The LMS ownership of the NCC is clearly displayed on the noticeboards on the platforms

However, permission was refused again because of an unauthorised level crossing and continuing problems with the River Bann bridge. Approval for opening was only given once the B&BR gave assurances that they would deal with the level crossing and complete the bridge within six months. The line duly opened for traffic on 10 November 1856. The line was not very profitable and in 1879 a competitor, the Great Northern Railway of Ireland, also arrived at Cookstown via Dungannon; the two companies' stations were adjacent to each other. In 1875, the Derry Central Railway was authorised to build a line from Magherafelt to Macfin. Opening on 19 February 1880, the new line made a junction at Magherafelt with the two lines running parallel for nearly half a mile before they parted company. During the construction of the DCR, another company was formed to build a line to Draperstown. The Draperstown Railway opened on 20 July 1883 and left the Cookstown line at Draperstown Junction, one and a quarter miles from Magherafelt.

A somewhat forlorn looking Moneymore Station, looking towards Cookstown.

At Cookstown a short spur continued on from the station, crossing Union Street on the level and terminating at the Market Yard. This part of the line was used for goods traffic and was usually worked by horse. There was also a connection to the GNR(I) line at Cookstown, used for wagon exchange. The B&BR became part of the Belfast & Northern Counties Railway on 15 May 1860 and subsequently part of the Midland Railway on 21 July 1903. The Second World War saw an upturn in traffic, not least with the establishment in July 1942 of a War Department store at Lisamoney, some one and a half miles before Moneymore. A Pinkerton Box guarded entry to the three-road reception yard and various spurs. A locomotive could be 'locked in' here for much of the day before working the marshalled train towards Antrim. The NCC was taken over by the Ulster Transport Authority on 1 April 1949 and on 28 August 1950 the whole line was closed to passenger traffic. Goods traffic continued until 2 May 1955 when the Magherafelt to Cookstown section was closed completely. However, the Cookstown line was used one more time as a UTA bus strike saw the running of a Sunday school excursion to Cookstown on 6 July 1955. The remaining section between Cookstown Junction, Toome Bridge and Magherafelt remained open for goods traffic, using the Derry Central route as far as Kilrea for another four years. This section closed completely on 5 November 1959.

Magherafelt – Macfin *

			Station closed	Date
Passenger service withdrawn	28 August 1950		Tamlaght Halt **	28 August 1950
Distance	29.25 miles		Kilrea	28 August 1950
Company	Northern Counties Committee		Garvagh	28 August 1950
			Moneycarrie Halt	28 August 1950
Stations closed		Date	Aghadowey	28 August 1950
Magherafelt		28 August 1950	Curragh Bridge Halt ***	28 August 1950
Knockloughrim		28 August 1950	Macfin	28 August 1950
Maghera		28 August 1950		
Upperlands		28 August 1950		

Maghera, 1937. Although this station lost its passenger services in 1950, goods trains continued to use the route as far as Kilrea until 1959.

A fertile agricultural area which had many small market towns and a number of linen mills, the Lower Bann Valley seemed ideal for a railway connection. In 1853 a scheme had been proposed in the form of the Dublin, Belfast & Coleraine Junction Railway which in part was intended to run between Magherafelt and Macfin. This came to nothing, but the neighbouring Belfast & Ballymena Railway did build a connecting branch to Randalstown in anticipation, extending to Cookstown in 1856. In the mid-1870s the Magherafelt to Macfin portion was proposed again and received its Act of incorporation on 11 August 1875. The Derry Central Railway was given running powers between Magherafelt Station and the junction of their line about half a mile away and also at the northern end of the line between Macfin and Coleraine. The line was to be worked by the BNCR.

* The closed station on this line that was in Co. Antrim was Macfin.   ** Opened in 1914.   *** Opened in 1908.

An unidentified 'light compound' passes through Upperlands Station with a mixed goods train. William Clarke's linen mill was served by a siding to the north of the station. The mill had its own internal 2 feet gauge horse-worked tramway which in latter years was worked by a mare called Fanny.

Due to difficulties in raising capital, work did not commence until 30 August 1877. The major engineering feature of the line was a 165 feet long bridge over the River Bann just south of Macfin. The bridge had a swing span to allow river traffic to pass. Continuing financial difficulties delayed the completion of the line and the company had to apply for a loan from the Board of Works. The line opened for business on 19 February 1880, but results were disappointing with the company unable to pay any dividend on shares. Despite the prosperity of the area, the DCR continued to have financial difficulties and a further loan was sought from the Board of Works in 1881. The end came on 4 April 1901 when the Board took possession of the line as a result of non-payment of interest, the debt having risen to £113,720 by this time. The line was handed over to the B&NCR who took full possession on the 17 August 1901. Two years later, the B&NCR became part of the Northern Counties Committee.

Kilrea Station on the Derry Central. The line was closed completely from Kilrea northwards to Macfin in 1950, the same year as the Derry Central lost its passenger services. Goods services survived from Magherafelt to Kilrea until that section closed completely nine years later.

The line continued as a backwater for much of its life, although it was a useful alternative to the main line via Ballymena. Special traffic catering for the local fairs (especially the one at Kilrea) kept the line going, but this traffic diminished greatly after the Second World War. Another important goods movement was the traffic to William Clarke's linen mill at Upperlands. At the north end of that station, a private siding ran across the village street on the level and continued on to the mills. The mill had a short 2 feet gauge railway which had been built around 1900 to connect the main works to the examining room. This crossed the broad gauge siding on the level and was worked by horse (in latter years by a mare called Fanny). The DCR became part of the Ulster Transport Authority on 1 April 1949 and the line lost its passenger service on 28 August 1950. The section from Kilrea north to Macfin also lost its goods services on the same day and this section closed completely. The remaining section from Magherafelt to Kilrea retained a daily goods service, mainly serving Clarke's mill, until this too closed on 5 October 1959.

Magherafelt – Draperstown

Passenger service withdrawn	1 October 1930	*Stations closed*	*Date*
Distance	8 miles	Magherafelt *	28 August 1950
Company	Northern Counties Committee	Desertmartin	1 October 1930
		Draperstown	1 October 1930

NCC A1 Class 4-4-0, No. 65, 'Knockagh', stands at Desertmartin Station, the only intermediate station on the Draperstown branch. In 1930 this became the first NCC broad gauge branch to lose its passenger services.

* This closed to Draperstown services on 1 October 1930, but remained open for Cookstown services until 28 August 1950.

The line had been closed to passenger services for seven years by the time this photograph was taken at Draperstown on 1 July 1937. Goods services survived until 1950 when the UTA closed the line completely.

The Draperstown Railway was incorporated on 2 July 1878 with the aim of building a line from Magherafelt to Draperstown. The company were to have running powers over the Belfast & Northern Counties Railway from Magherafelt to Draperstown Junction and then would run on their own line to the terminus. Construction started in late 1881 and was ready for inspection by mid-1883. The line was originally intended to have just one station, although a decision in late 1882 provided for an intermediate station at Desertmartin, five miles from Draperstown. The line opened to passenger traffic on 20 July 1883 and was worked by the B&NCR. Goods traffic commenced on 8 October 1883. The company was in financial difficulties from the start, having to borrow money from the Board of Works. Despite this it still ended up with a bank overdraft and quite a debt of interest on the loan. As a result of these mounting debts, the Board of Works forced the sale of the line to the B&NCR, possession being confirmed in the Act of July 1895. The line became part of the Northern Counties Committee system in 1903. Passenger trains were finally withdrawn on 1 October 1930, making this the first NCC broad gauge line to lose them, although goods services continued. In 1942 a US Army motor transport depot was established at Luney Camp and this was served by a three-quarter mile siding which left the line about half a mile from Draperstown Junction. This siding lasted until 1945. The end of the line finally came when the Ulster Transport Authority closed its goods services on 3 July 1950.

Magilligan – Magilligan Point

Passenger service withdrawn	October 1855	*Stations closed*	*Date*
Distance	4.5 miles	Magilligan	October 1855
Company	Londonderry & Coleraine Railway	Drummond	October 1855
		Magilligan Point	October 1855

Magilligan Station on the Coleraine to Londonderry line, looking west. The short-lived branch to Magilligan Point commenced here. The line to Londonderry is still open, although Magilligan was finally closed some time in the 1980s.

In operation for just five months, this line was the shortest lived passenger line in Ireland. When the Londonderry & Coleraine Railway were busy building their route between these two towns in the early 1850s they provided a station for the small town of Magilligan. At this point there is a promontory which juts out into the sea, ending very near the Donegal coast. A branch was built from Magilligan to Magilligan Point with the hope of introducing a ferry service to Greencastle in Donegal. No parliamentary powers were sought for the four and a half mile branch and the land was given free by the landowner. It seems that the Board of Trade were also unaware of the new line. Work began in September 1853 and was complete by 1855, however there was no Board of Trade inspection or an official opening of the branch. The only sign that it had opened for business was an entry in the July 1855 edition of Bradshaw, so it is assumed the line opened at the end of June or the beginning of July.

It appears that the line was unprofitable and it is believed that the branch had stopped running by October 1855. The next mention of it is in a report to the shareholders in December 1856 where it is stated that the line was unremunerative and had been abandoned. It appears that the line may have been built in a different gauge to the main line, namely the British Standard Gauge of 4 feet 8.5 inches, although there is no direct evidence of this. The generous time of forty minutes given to traverse the four and a half miles indicates that the line was probably worked by horse.

Limavady Junction – Dungiven

		Stations closed	Date
Passenger service withdrawn	1 January 1933 (Limavady to Dungiven) / 2 May 1955 (Limavady Junction to Limavady)	Limavady Junction *	18 October 1976
		Broighter **	3 July 1950
		Limavady ***	3 July 1950
Distance	13.5 miles	Ardmore	1 January 1933
Company	Northern Counties Committee	Drumsurn	1 January 1933
		Derryork	1 January 1933
		Dungiven	1 January 1933

The 11.37 a.m. departure to Limavady stands at Limavady Junction, 19 April 1948. An unidentified U2 Class 4-4-0 is in charge of carriages 216 and 79 for the three and a quarter mile run.

* Opened in July 1853 as Junction, then renamed as Newtown Junction from 1861 to 1875. It became Limavady Junction in 1876. It closed as a junction station on 3 July 1950, but remained open for main line passenger services until 1976.
** Opened in February 1853. Not advertised as a stop from the 1920s to 1 June 1934.
*** Called Newtown-limavady until 1870.

Limavady Junction, looking east, with a fine array of somersault signals. The Limavady branch can be seen curving away to the right. Although the branch lost its passenger services in 1950, the station continued to be served by main line trains until 1976.

The branch started off life as part of the Londonderry & Coleraine Railway's original plan to connect Londonderry and Coleraine. The LCR was authorised on 4 August 1845 to build thirty miles of main line railway and a four mile branch to Limavady. Considerable engineering work was required as numerous embankments and land reclamation schemes were involved. After a difficult seven years, which saw the LCR dissolved and reformed twice, the first section of line between Londonderry and Limavady was ready for use in September 1852.

NCC U1 Class 4-4-0, No. 4A, 'Glenariff', stands at Limavady Station, 22 April 1948. Built in 1931 by the NCC, 4A had only one more year to go before being withdrawn.

Following a Board of Trade inspection the line was opened for goods traffic in October 1852, but the Board was unhappy with the running of passenger trains until some additional work had been carried out. Eventually they gave authorisation and passenger services commenced on 29 December 1852. Meanwhile, work was still progressing on the section to Coleraine which started at Broharris Junction, four miles from Limavady. It was opened to all traffic on 18 July 1853, leaving Limavady at the end of a three and a quarter mile branch. However, in those early days all train services served Limavady. As there was no platform at Broharris Junction, the trains would proceed to Limavady and then reverse back before carrying on along the main line.

Limavady Station became the terminus for passenger services on the Dungiven branch in 1933, although goods services continued to Dungiven until 1950. Limavady was also closed to passengers in 1950, but its goods services continued until the closure of the line in 1955.

Continuing financial difficulties found the LCR being leased to the neighbouring Belfast & Northern Counties Railway in 1861, the BNCR eventually buying the LCR on 24 July 1871. Ten miles to the south of Limavady is the town of Dungiven, in the estate of the Skinner's Company. Although an extension had been thought of in 1862, it was not until during extensive reconstruction and improving of the town in the 1870s that serious thought was given to a railway connection. The Limavady & Dungiven Railway Act was passed on 4 July 1878 with the intention of building a line from the existing station at Limavady to Dungiven, via Ardmore, Drumsurn and Derryork.

Dungiven Station pictured in 1937, four years after it lost its passenger service. Never a profitable line, this was the second broad gauge line closed to passengers by the NCC.

The company was in financial difficulties from the start, a Board of Works loan being required before the contractors could build the railway. The line opened for all traffic on the 4 July 1883, being worked by the B&NCR from the outset. Mounting debts of interest on the Board of Works loan saw the Board taking possession of the Limavady & Dungiven Railway in 1907 and its consequent sale to the NCC on 9 August 1907. Continuing poor receipts ensured that the Limavady to Dungiven section lost its passenger service on 1 January 1933, although goods services continued.

An unidentified locomotive shunts wagons at Dungiven Station.

The NCC became part of the UTA in 1949 and it wasn't too long before the rest of the line disappeared. Goods services between Limavady and Dungiven ceased on 3 July 1950, resulting in the total closure of this section. The same day passenger services ceased between Limavady Junction and Limavady. Goods services continued on the remaining part of the line for another five years, until that too was closed on 2 May 1955.

Desertone Halt – Londonderry Victoria Road

Passenger service withdrawn	1 January 1955	*Stations closed*	*Date*
Distance	14.5 miles	Desertone Halt *	1 January 1955
Company	Northern Counties Committee	New Buildings	1 January 1955
		Londonderry Victoria Road	1 January 1955

New Buildings Station on the UTA narrow gauge route from Strabane to Londonderry, 20 April 1953.

The narrow gauge railways in Co. Donegal, eventually known as the Co. Donegal Railways Joint Committee, converged at Strabane. Here there was an interchange with the Great Northern Railway of Ireland, with passengers having to change platforms and goods being transhipped between broad and narrow gauges before reaching their destinations. It is not particularly surprising therefore that a scheme was promoted in the 1890s to build a narrow gauge line from Strabane to Londonderry. The proposal met with stiff opposition from the GNR(I) who claimed that the line would duplicate their existing route, but despite the opposition an Act was obtained in 1896 for the Donegal Railway to build its own line to Londonderry. Its fourteen and a half mile line was opened for goods traffic on 1 August 1900 and for passengers a few days later on 6 August 1900.

* Opened in 1908.

2-6-4T, No. 17, 'Glenties', arrives at Londonderry Victoria Road with a train from Strabane, 24 June 1937.

Leaving Strabane, the line continued north for a short distance before turning north-east to cross over the GNR(I) line and to continue up the east side of the River Foyle through the counties of Tyrone and 'Derry. The Donegal Railway terminus in Londonderry was at Victoria Road, a short distance south of the BNCR Waterside station and next to the Craigavon Bridge. The Londonderry Port & Harbour Commissioners built their own mixed gauge railway, connecting the Donegal Railway with the BNCR to the north, and across the lower deck of the bridge to the West Bank. Here, connections were made to the GNR(I) Foyle Road station and to the Londonderry & Lough Swilly Railways Graving Dock station.

With the Craigavon Bridge in the background, CDRJC 5 Class 2-6-4T, No. 19, 'Letterkenny', stands at the head of the 10.00 a.m. departure from Victoria Road to Strabane, 23 June 1937.

In 1903 the English Midland Railway entered the scene when they purchased the Belfast & Northern Counties Railway. Keen to expand elsewhere, the MR approached the Donegal Railway with a view to purchasing it. Alarmed at the prospect, the GNR(I) understandably objected to the proposal. Agreement was finally reached in 1906 whereby both the GNR(I) and the MR jointly purchased the company and set up the Co. Donegal Railways Joint Committee to manage the system. However, Parliament was concerned that the GNR(I) would have a monopoly on the Londonderry to Strabane route and consequently the narrow gauge route passed entirely to the Midland Railway Northern Counties Committee, with the line being worked by the CDRJC. The MR NCC became the LMS NCC in 1924.

Although owned by the UTA since 1949, trains from Londonderry Victoria Road to Strabane were worked by the CDRJC. In the picture CDRJC 2-6-4T 5 Class, No. 8, 'Foyle', built by Nasmyth, Wilson in 1907, makes ready with the 10.00 a.m. to Strabane, 20 April 1953.

The fortunes of the CDRJC started to decline in the years between the wars despite various economies put into action, including the extensive introduction of railcars. The Second World War had more of an effect on the line. Londonderry became an important naval base and generated a lot of war traffic. However, this traffic was routed over the NCC route to Waterside station via Coleraine. The GNR(I) route was not used as it passed through several miles of neutral Eire and the narrow gauge was considered unsuitable because of transhipment difficulties at Strabane. The NCC passed to the control of the Ulster Transport Authority on 1 April 1949, although the line continued to be worked by the CDRJC. In October 1954 the UTA issued a notice stating their intentions to withdraw services on the line and it closed to all traffic on 1 January 1955. However, due to a UTA bus strike one train, carrying a Sunday school excursion, was run on 30 June 1955 from Strabane to Portrush.

Portstewart Tramway

Passenger service withdrawn	31 October 1926	*Station closed*	*Date*
Distance	1.75 miles	Golf Links Halt (request stop)	31 January 1926
Company	Northern Counties Committee	Victoria Terrace	31 January 1926
		Parade *	31 January 1926
Stations closed	*Date*	Portstewart Town	31 January 1926
Portstewart Station	31 January 1926		
Millbank (request stop)	31 January 1926	* Later called Promenade.	

The tram terminus at Portstewart, informally known as Montagu Arms Hotel. The depot was a short distance from the terminus. Fortunately, one locomotive, No. 2, has survived and is preserved at the transport museum at Cultra near Belfast.

Tram locomotive No. 3, built in 1900, at Portstewart. The vehicle behind the locomotive is the four-wheeled 'toastrack' car which was supplied new in 1882. To comply with railway regulations, the locomotives were fitted with side skirts and condensing apparatus.

Due to opposition by local landowners, the Belfast, Ballymena, Coleraine & Portrush Junction Railway bypassed the town of Portstewart when they opened their line to Portrush in 1855. A station was opened in 1856 to serve the town, but was actually two miles away. However, the local inhabitants of this small seaside town were keen to get connected to the railway system, especially when they saw the effect the railway had on the neighbouring resort of Portrush.

A tram at Victoria Terrace, Portstewart. Opened in 1882, the tramway had a relatively short life, closing in 1926.

A scheme was launched in 1861 to connect the town and the station by a roadside tramway, but this failed due to continuing opposition by landowners. Eventually the landowners changed their minds and another scheme was considered in 1871, this time being a broad gauge light railway. However, the BNCR was not interested in building or operating the line, so again nothing happened.

A well-loaded tram stands at Victoria Terrace in Midland Railway days. Three 0-4-0T locomotives were supplied by Kitson and Co. of Leeds between 1882 and 1900. The locomotive is hauling a four-wheel luggage van and the open-top double-decker tramcar.

The scheme was revived once more in 1879 as a 3 foot gauge tramway and on 26 April 1880 the Portstewart Tramway Company was formed. The tramway was to follow the country road from Portstewart Station to the town. The line was single throughout, but had two passing loops. The official opening took place on 28 June 1882 and initial results looked promising. However, the company soon ran into financial difficulties and was declared bankrupt on 15 October 1892.

After the closure of the Portstewart Tramway, the NCC ran a replacement bus service. Here, NCC bus number 102 stands at Portstewart, 15 July 1933.

Nonetheless, it carried on until early 1897 when proceedings were taken to wind it up and sell it as a going concern. The BNCR bought the line on 1 June 1897, but due to its rundown condition they had to go to considerable expense to get the line back up to standard. A new depot was built at Portstewart in 1899 and in 1903 a new loop and shelter were built at Victoria Terrace with some services terminating there.

NCC U2 Class 4-4-0, No. 71, 'Glenarm Castle' stands at Portstewart Station, 1933. The tramway started outside in the station yard. Although the Portrush branch is still in use, this station closed in 1988.

The Midland Railway bought the BNCR in 1903 and so the tramway came under NCC control. However, it continued to lose money and in October 1925 the decision was taken to close it. Services ceased on 31 January 1926.

Strabane – Londonderry Foyle Road *

Passenger service withdrawn	15 February 1965	*Stations closed*	*Date*
Distance	14.75 miles	Londonderry Cow Market	1850
Company	Great Northern Railway of Ireland	Londonderry Gallows Strand **	date unknown
		Londonderry Foyle Road ***	15 February 1965

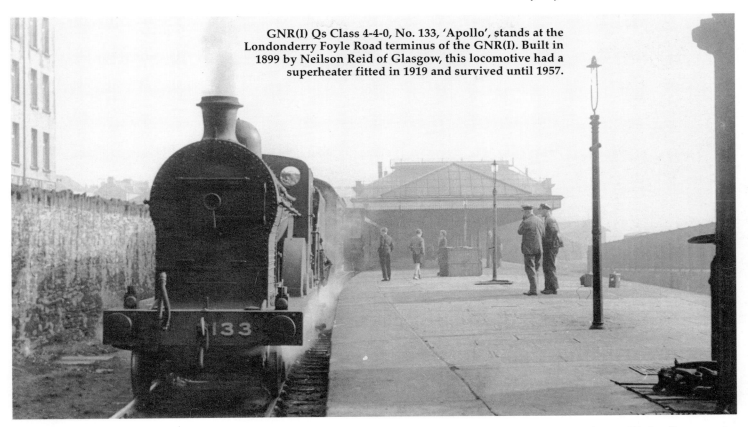

GNR(I) Qs Class 4-4-0, No. 133, 'Apollo', stands at the Londonderry Foyle Road terminus of the GNR(I). Built in 1899 by Neilson Reid of Glasgow, this locomotive had a superheater fitted in 1919 and survived until 1957.

* The closed station on this line that was in Co. Tyrone was Strabane. The closed stations that were in Co. Donegal were Porthall, Carrickmore, St Johnston and Carrigans. ** Closed after the extension to the Foyle Road terminus opened; exact date unknown. *** Opened on 18 April 1850.

With only one station actually in Co. 'Derry, Foyle Road Station was the terminus of the Great Northern Railway of Ireland's routes from Belfast and Dundalk. The two routes converged at Omagh in Co. Tyrone and the line continued northwards through Strabane before crossing into Co. Donegal. It then ran up the west bank of the River Foyle and eventually crossed into Co. 'Derry just north of Carrigans Station.

GNR(I) PP Class 4-4-0, No. 70, at Londonderry Foyle Road. Built in 1896 by Beyer, Peacock, this locomotive survived almost to the end of the GNR(I), being withdrawn in 1957.

The line was originally built by the Londonderry & Enniskillen Railway (L&ER) which was incorporated in July 1845 and authorised to build a line from Londonderry to Enniskillen via Strabane and Omagh. Construction started in October 1845, with the first section to Strabane down the west bank of the River Foyle being completed and opened on 19 April 1847. The siting of the Londonderry terminus was subject to some difference of opinion and was originally built at Gallows Strand. This site was found to be somewhat inconvenient and an extension, opening on 18 April 1850, was made towards the city to a site just north of the Carlisle Bridge, known as Foyle Road from 1904. Initial results were so poor that in 1848 the L&ER board tried to abandon the rest of the line. However, the company carried on pushing southwards, opening the line in stages as each section was completed. The L&ER eventually reached Enniskillen in 1854. Meanwhile, another concern in the form of the Dundalk & Enniskillen Railway (D&ER) was busy pushing north to meet the L&ER at Enniskillen. This was achieved in 1859 and it soon became apparent to the board of the L&ER that the complete route would be better run as one concern. So, from 1 January 1860, the L&ER leased their line to the D&ER for ninety-nine years. The D&ER changed their name to the Irish North Western Railway (INWR) by act of Parliament on 7 July 1862.

GNR(I) AL Class 0-6-0, No. 140, receives attention at the coaling stage at the shed just to the south of Londonderry Foyle Road Station, 19 April 1948.

In the meantime, the Portadown, Dungannon & Omagh Railway had reached Omagh, opening their line on 2 September 1861. This new line offered an alternative route from Belfast to Londonderry. 1875 saw the formation of the Northern Railway of Ireland (NR(I)), the INWR joining the fold on 1 January 1876, with the L&ER remaining independent for the time being; however, the lease was transferred to the NR(I). The NR(I) was a short-lived company, ending on 1 April 1876 when the Ulster Railway amalgamated with it to form the Great Northern Railway of Ireland. The still independent L&ER eventually promoted a Bill for amalgamation with the GNR(I) and joined the fold in 1883. Partition in 1921 caused numerous problems for the GNR(I), with the line commencing in the Irish Free State and terminating in Northern Ireland. Along the way, the line crossed the state border three times, at Clones, Strabane and Carrigans. Customs posts were set up at Clones in the Irish Free State and Newtownbutler in Northern Ireland.

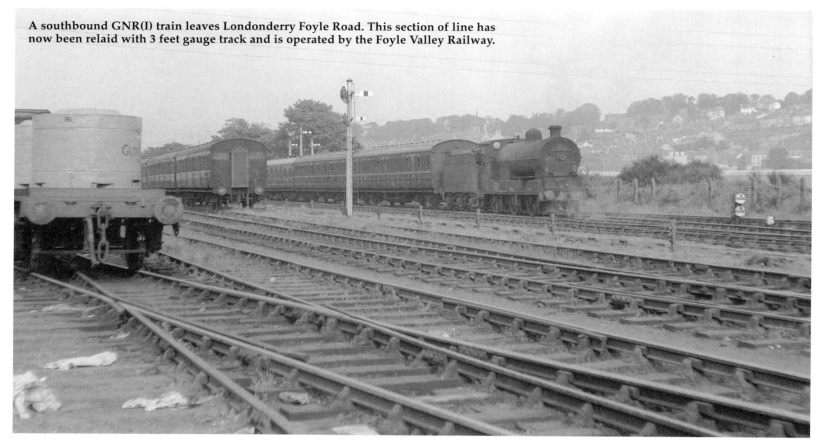

A southbound GNR(I) train leaves Londonderry Foyle Road. This section of line has now been relaid with 3 feet gauge track and is operated by the Foyle Valley Railway.

The 1920s also heralded another threat to the line in the form of competing road transport. Profits began to fall, becoming a loss in 1933. The Railway Strike of 1933 didn't help matters and the GNR(I) looked for economies. One of these was in the form of railcars, introduced on the line in 1935. As well as serving the established stations, the railcars would also stop at numerous level crossings in an effort to pick up extra traffic. The Second World War saw the economic situation improve for the GNR(I), but caused problems for this particular line. Since the line crossed the state border War Department traffic would have had to pass through neutral Eire on its way to the major naval base of Londonderry. Instead, this traffic went on the NCC route via Coleraine. The immediate post-war years saw a return to financial difficulties. In 1953, the governments of the two countries set up the Great Northern Railway Board, underwriting the losses of the railway. In 1956, the Northern Minister of Commerce proposed a radical closure programme, including the Omagh to Newtownbutler section of the Irish North. Although these proposals were initially opposed, a public enquiry was held.

The GNR(I) goods depot at Londonderry. Foyle Road Station is just behind the position of the photographer and the engine shed is about half a mile away in the other direction.

The outcome of the enquiry revealed that minimal savings would be achieved, but despite this the closure went ahead with services ceasing at the end of September 1957. All services between Clones and Omagh stopped on 1 October 1957, leaving the Omagh to Londonderry section in use as part of the route from Belfast to Londonderry via Portadown. A year later saw the demise of the GNRB, with the company ceasing to exist from midnight on 30 September 1958. The Ulster Transport Authority acquired the assets of the company in Northern Ireland. They continued to operate services over the remaining part of the line between Omagh and Londonderry until they finally closed the Portadown to Londonderry route on 15 February 1965. This isn't quite the end of the story. In 1977 a preservation group called the Foyle Valley Railway acquired a site just to the south of the former GNR(I) station site in Londonderry. A museum has been built and a 3 feet gauge line has been laid on the former trackbed, running three miles to the south. Services are operated by two former Co. Donegal railcars and it is hoped that the line will extended further south and across the border.

Londonderry Middle Quay – Tooban Junction *

Passenger service withdrawn	1 June 1888
	(Londonderry Middle Quay to Graving Dock) /
	9 August 1953
	(Londonderry Graving Dock to Tooban Junction)
Distance	7.25 miles
Company	Londonderry & Lough Swilly Railway

Stations closed	*Date*
Londonderry Middle Quay **	1 June 1888
Londonderry Graving Dock	9 August 1953
Pennyburn Halt	1888
Gallagh Road	9 August 1953
Harrity's Road	1864

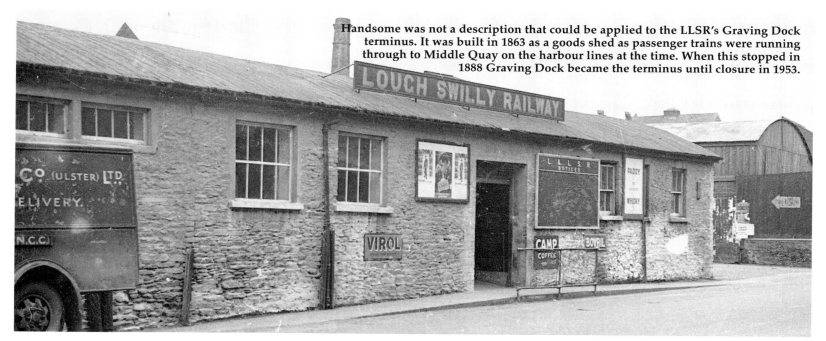

Handsome was not a description that could be applied to the LLSR's Graving Dock terminus. It was built in 1863 as a goods shed as passenger trains were running through to Middle Quay on the harbour lines at the time. When this stopped in 1888 Graving Dock became the terminus until closure in 1953.

The Lough Foyle & Lough Swilly Railway Company was registered in 1852 to build a railway from Londonderry to Farland Point. This eight and three-quarter mile long railway was intended to tap into the low-lying fertile areas of East Donegal and a connecting boat service from a small pier at Farland Point that would sail to various other destinations on Lough Swilly.

* The closed stations on this line that were in Co. Donegal were Bridge End, Burnfoot and Tooban Junction.
** The Londonderry & Lough Swilly Railway used the Londonderry Port & Harbour Commissioners' station and line at Middle Quay between 1 January 1869 and 3 January 1885 and again between 1 July 1885 and 1 January 1888.

A Kerr, Stuart 4-6-2T, No. 10, originally named 'Richmond', ready to depart Graving Dock Station with the 3.30 p.m. to Buncrana, 19 April 1948.

The company was authorised on 26 June 1853 and had in the meantime changed its name to the more familiar Londonderry & Lough Swilly Railway (LLSR). Difficulty in raising capital meant that another Act of 1 August 1859 was needed before construction started. Built to the Irish Standard Gauge of 5 feet 3 inches, the line was inspected by the Board of Trade in October 1863, but it was unhappy with a couple of features of the line, including three unauthorised level crossings that had to be replaced with bridges. The LLSR gave an undertaking to build these bridges within twelve months and duly opened the line on 31 December 1863. As it turned out, these bridges were never built. Another interesting condition imposed on the LLSR concerned the road crossing at Pennyburn where the line had to cross the road at an angle to gain access to the terminus station at Graving Dock. As this was a busy road it was decided that trains should not be hauled by any mechanical means, but only by animals. However, apart from a period in early 1864 when horses were used, the condition was ignored and steam locomotives worked trains across the crossing totally illegally for fifty-five years until an Act of 21 November 1918 officially gave them powers to do so.

Graving Dock was also the goods terminus of the LLSR. Here, 4-6-2T, No. 15, arrives with a goods train from Letterkenny on 19 April 1948. Built in 1899 by Hudswell, Clarke, the locomotive was originally numbered 5, but was renumbered 15 in 1913.

While the Farland Point line was being constructed, the LLSR decided to build another line up the east bank of Lough Swilly to Fahan and on to Buncrana. An Act of 22 July 1861 authorised the company to make a junction with their existing line at what later became known as Tooban Junction. The line was to then run north to Fahan and Buncrana. It opened on 8 September 1864 and effectively left the Farland Point line as a branch; a shortage of locomotives also left this to be worked by horses until it closed completely in June 1866 and was lifted in 1877. Back in Londonderry, the company were concerned at their Graving Dock terminus being over a mile from the city centre and were keen to get their passengers closer to the centre. As a result, in 1869 they arranged with the Londonderry Port & Harbour Commissioners to use their harbour line as far as Middle Quay where a platform had been erected.

LLSR No. 2, a 4-6-0T built by Andrew Barclay in 1902 for the Londonderry & Burtonport Extension Railway, is pictured entering Pennyburn, having just crossed the Strand Road level crossing with an excursion train from Londonderry Graving Dock to Buncrana, 24 June 1937.

Meanwhile, plans were afoot to connect the important Donegal town of Letterkenny to Londonderry. Various schemes and routes were proposed before the Letterkenny Railway was authorised by an Act of 3 July 1860 to build an Irish Standard Gauge line to connect with the nearby Londonderry & Enniskillen Railway at Cuttymanhill just to the south of St Johnstown, seven miles south of Londonderry. However, three years passed and nothing was done. An amendment to the Act on 13 July 1863 altered the course of the Letterkenny Railway to run into Londonderry via the LLSR's route from Farland Point, with the management and working of the line to be given to the LLSR. Although construction started, money soon ran out and a further act of 1866 was required to raise further capital. However, this failed to materialise, construction stopped and the line lay derelict. Various attempts were made over the next few years to raise the money by rearranging the capital and finally this resulted in the company arranging a mortgage in three parts. An Act of 1876 authorised the financial restructuring and contractors were sought to complete the line. However, the line had lain derelict for ten years and the lowest tender made it clear that the line could not be completed as envisaged.

Pennyburn Halt was provided mainly for use by railway staff and most trains called there. No. 1, a 4-6-0T built by Andrew Barclay in 1902 for the Londonderry & Burtonport Extension Railway, pauses with a train from Buncrana, 6 August 1930.

The contracting firm of McCrea & McFarland suggested a change to 3 feet gauge and the proposal met with the approval of the Letterkenny Railway board and a Bill was put before Parliament. The Bill became an Act on 29 June 1880 and also gave the Swilly Railway authority to re-gauge their line so that the whole line could be worked as one. Construction on the Letterkenny Railway recommenced in May 1881 and the LLSR commenced the laying of 3 feet gauge track from Tooban Junction westwards to meet the Letterkenny Railway at a point known as Burt Junction. This was not actually a junction as such because the two lines met end on; it was really a boundary point between the two companies' property. The line opened for business on 30 June 1883 and for a couple of years, Tooban Junction had both broad and narrow gauge trains serving it, although passengers for Londonderry had to change trains and gauge to reach their destination. Obviously, it wasn't long before consideration was given to re-gauging the Buncrana line and this was begun on the evening of 28 March 1885 and completed within a week. This led to an interesting situation at Londonderry.

The locomotive shed at Pennyburn, 18 April 1948. This was the main shed of the LLSR where most of the maintenance was carried out.

The LLSR still continued to run their trains to Middle Quay, over the LP&HC lines, although now one had the unusual sight of narrow gauge trains being hauled by broad gauge locomotives over mixed gauge track. The working ceased on 1 January 1888. As it happened, this was yet another illegal practice the LLSR had been involved in as neither company had official authority to run passenger trains over the harbour lines. The LLSR company went on to extend their influence both to the north and west. The northern extension continued on from Buncrana to Cardonagh and opened on 1 July 1901. The western extension was officially the Letterkenny & Burtonport Extension Railway (LBER) and opened on 9 March 1903. Both extensions were built with government grants. Partition in 1921 found the LLSR operating in two different political states and was to have a profound effect on the company's finances. The company remained independent but saw traffic flows change to reflect the new political boundaries as well as suffering the delays caused by customs examinations. It started to lose money in 1925 and was kept afloat with grants from both governments.

Looking out of the city, Pennyburn Halt is on the left with the locomotive shed opposite, 19 May 1950. Just outside the shed is one of the enormous 4-8-4 tanks built by Hudswell, Clarke in 1912. This wheel arrangement was unique in the British Isles.

An approach was made by the LLSR to the neighbouring Co. Donegal Railways to take over the working of the system, but this was declined, as was a similar approach made by the government of Northern Ireland in 1930. As a result the company started to close some of its lines with the Carndonagh extension closing on 2 December 1935 and Buncrana being left with a limited service. The Burtonport Extension lost its services completely on 3 July 1940 with only a goods service continuing as far as Letterkenny. However, wartime restrictions and public protests resulted in a restoration of goods services to Gweedore in 1941 followed by passenger services from March 1942. Buncrana had its passenger service restored in 1942. The reprieve lasted until just after the war when the Letterkenny–Gweedore section closed completely on 6 January 1947. The remaining services continued up until 1953, the Letterkenny service going on 1 July 1953 and the Buncrana service on 10 August 1953. The company had got into road transport in the 1920s, operating both bus and lorry services in the area. Long after the company had stopped running railway services, it was possible to see these vehicles carrying the logo of the LLSR.

Londonderry Port & Harbour Commissioners

The LP&HC ran three steam locomotives on their dock lines on the west bank of the River Foyle. No. 1, an 0-6-0ST built by Robert Stephenson in 1891, survived until the closure of the system in 1962. Note the mixed gauge track and the two types of couplings on the buffer beam.

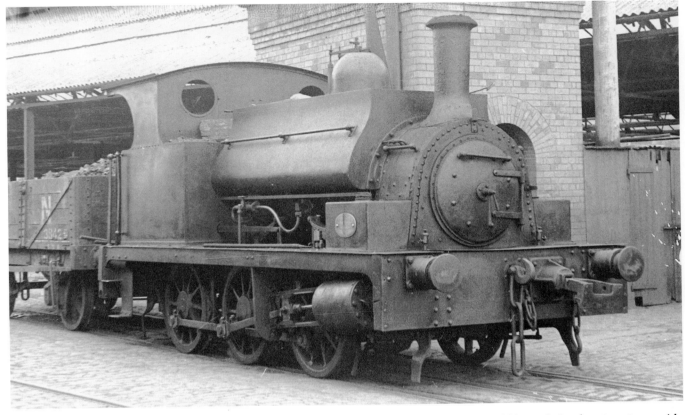

Although not a passenger carrier as such, the Londonderry Port & Harbour Commissioners soon realised that it would be to their advantage to provide rail connections between the various railway companies and their docks. In 1863 a new bridge was provided across the River Foyle and was equipped with two decks. The upper deck of the Carlisle Bridge carried road traffic while the lower deck carried the 5 feet 3 inch gauge harbour line from the Belfast & Northern Counties (BNCR) station at Waterside across the river to the west bank of the Foyle. Further connections were made with the GNR(I) at Foyle Road Station and the LLSR at Graving Dock. From 1869 the LLSR were using the harbour line for passenger services to a station at Middle Quay. The BNCR built a new goods depot on the west bank just to the north of Foyle Road station and Londonderry City Goods, as it was known, opened in 1877. The bridge was at right angles to railway lines and, as such, access to the bridge was by means of wagon turntables. Wagons were hauled across the bridge by the use of capstans and horses as locomotives were prohibited.

The lower deck of the Craigavon Bridge was laid with mixed gauge track to enable wagon transfers between the NCC, GNR(I), LLSR and Donegal railways. As the bridge was at right angles to the railway lines, access was by means of wagon turntables. Operated by the LP&HC, wagons were hauled across by horse and capstan.

The LLSR changed their gauge to 3 feet in 1885 and an additional rail was laid to produce the mixed gauge system. This led to the unusual sight of narrow gauge trains being hauled by the LP&HC broad gauge locomotives from Graving Dock to Middle Quay over mixed gauge track. The working ceased on 1 January 1888. As it happened, this was an illegal practice as neither company had official authority to run passenger trains over the harbour lines. In 1900 the Co. Donegal Railway reached Londonderry with a station on the east bank at Victoria Road. The LP&HC provided a narrow gauge connection to the Donegal. The LH&PC only had broad gauge locomotives to haul trains of both gauges. As such, the buffer beam of the locomotives carried both a conventional drawhook and three link coupling as well as a narrow gauge 'chopper' coupling which was lower down and slightly offset. The Carlisle Bridge was replaced in 1933 by the Craigavon Bridge, the new bridge still retaining the twin deck layout with the lower deck allocated for rail use. The LLSR closed in 1953 and the former Donegal station closed in 1955, leaving the LP&HC with a purely broad gauge operation. Falling traffic saw the closure of the system in 1962. The lower deck of the bridge was converted for use by road vehicles. Fortunately, one of the locomotives survives in preservation.

Closed passenger stations on lines still open to passengers

Coleraine – Londonderry

Line/Service	Date
Station closed	**Date**
Coleraine Waterside	1861
Barmouth	1856
Downhill	18 October 1976
Umbra	1861?
Magilligan	1980s
Limavady Junction	18 October 1976
Drennan's Farm *	1940s

Station closed	Date
Ballykelly	20 September 1954
Carrichue	20 September 1954
Faughanvale	1859
Longfield *	1940s
Eglinton	2 July 1973
Culmore	2 July 1973
Lisahally *	1940s
Londonderry Waterside **	24 February 1980

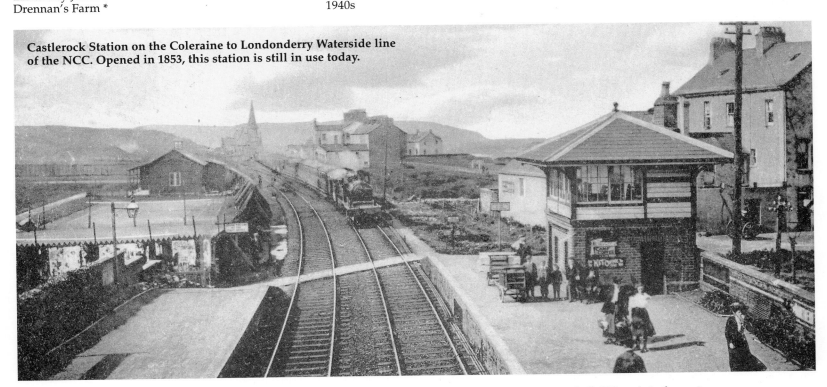

Castlerock Station on the Coleraine to Londonderry Waterside line of the NCC. Opened in 1853, this station is still in use today.

* These stations were military halts in use during the Second World War.

** A new station was built 200 yards to the west.

Downhill Station, looking east. Closed in 1976, this station was on the NCC route from Belfast York Road to Londonderry Waterside. In the distance is Downhill Tunnel and on top of the hill is Mussenden Temple.

Completed in 1875, Londonderry Waterside Station replaced an earlier station on the same site. The clock faces were added to the Italianate tower in 1888. This station was closed in 1980 and replaced by a new station 200 yards to the west.

Showing its LMS heritage, NCC W Class Mogul, No. 95, 'The Braid', stands at the head of the 11.10 a.m. departure from Londonderry Waterside to Belfast York Road, 19 April 1948.

WT Class 2-6-4T, No. 52, heads the 8.30 a.m. departure from Londonderry Waterside to Belfast York Road, 20 May 1950. Although No. 52 is displaying NCC on its tanks, the locomotive had passed to the UTA in 1949.